General

BIBLE SMUGGLER

THE STORY OF BROTHER ANDREW

David Wallington

RELIGIOUS AND MORAL EDUCATION PRESS
An Imprint of Arnold-Wheaton

Religious and Moral Education Press
Hennock Road, Exeter EX2 8RP
An Imprint of Arnold-Wheaton

A Division of E. J. Arnold & Son Ltd
Parkside Lane, Leeds LS11 5TD

A subsidiary of Pergamon Press Ltd
Headington Hill Hall, Oxford OX3 0BW

Pergamon Press Inc.
Maxwell House, Fairview Park, Elmsford, New York 10523

Pergamon Press Canada Ltd
Suite 104, 150 Consumers Road, Willowdale, Ontario M2J 1P9

Pergamon Press (Australia) Pty Ltd
P.O. Box 544, Potts Point, N.S.W. 2011

Pergamon Press GmbH
Hammerweg 6, D-6242 Kronberg, Federal Republic of Germany

Photographs are reproduced by courtesy of Keston College (p.15),
Novesti Press Agency (p.10) and "Open Doors" (pp.18, 19, 21).
Cover photograph by courtesy of the Revd J. Innes.

First published 1979

Reprinted 1981, 1985

Printed in Great Britain by A. Wheaton & Co. Ltd, Hennock Road, Exeter

ISBN 0 08-024159-X *non net*
ISBN 0 08-024160-3 *net*

BIBLE SMUGGLER

The story of Brother Andrew

"Halt!" shouted the German sentry as he heard a noise in the dark. But it was too late. There was a flash and a loud bang right outside the commander's house.

After letting off the firework young Andrew raced up the main street of the little Dutch village. As the guards chased him he heard the clicking of rifle-bolts. His heart missed a beat. He threw himself on the ground in the middle of a cabbage-patch in one of the gardens beside the road.

The guards hunted in the dark for an hour, then finally gave up in disgust. Andrew was safe. Once again he had outwitted the hated German soldiers who were occupying the country – Holland.

The war had come to his village, about twenty miles north of Amsterdam, when Andrew was twelve years old. On 10 May 1940 the Germans bombed and invaded Holland without warning. The Dutch army fought bravely, but in the end they had to give in. Now there were German soldiers in every Dutch village and town. Andrew wanted to show them that they were not welcome.

Of course, he could only annoy them. Sometimes it was with fireworks. Sometimes he managed to get at the German commander's car. The next morning, for some strange reason, it simply would not start.

But gradually things became worse. Many young Dutchmen were taken away to become slave-workers for the Germans. Sometimes the soldiers came to his village looking for more. Andrew and his friends had to run for their lives across the flat Dutch fields, ducking low not to be seen. Then they dived into a canal and swam to a safe spot.

Andrew also had to give up annoying the Germans. In another village, when the Germans were angry about something, they simply lined up a number of innocent people who had done nothing, and shot them. Andrew did not want to get someone else killed.

At long last the war came to an end. Andrew was seventeen years old. His father, the village blacksmith, told him he must find a job.

Andrew as a soldier

After the war against Germany, for a short time the Dutch fought another war in the Far East. It was in the country which is today called Indonesia. This used to be a Dutch colony, and rebels were fighting the Dutch army there.

Seeking adventure, Andrew joined the Dutch army. He was fit and strong, and not afraid of anybody. He loved the training, especially as he was chosen to belong to a special commando unit.

By Christmas 1946 he found himself in the beautiful land of Indonesia. At first he enjoyed it. However, when all their training was completed, Andrew's unit had to go into battle.

Suddenly Andrew found that he hated being a soldier. It was not the danger – he found that exciting. No, it was having to kill people. Instead of target practice, they were shooting real people.

2

Once they were marching through a village when some mines placed in the ground began to explode. It was a trap. Some of the Dutch soldiers were badly hurt. The rest, terrified and angry, began to shoot anyone on sight. In the end, women and children, as well as unarmed men, lay dead.

When it was all over, Andrew was horrified at his part in it. The Dutch soldiers had killed innocent people, just like the Germans had done.

From that moment Andrew began to hate himself. When he was in battle he did not care if he got killed. He even wore a bright yellow straw hat, inviting the enemy to shoot at him.

When he was not fighting he used to get drunk with his friends. They had a motto: "Be smart. Go crazy!" The reason for all this was that deep down Andrew and the others felt guilty for the awful things they had done in the war.

At home in Holland Andrew used to go to church with his family, but not now. His girl-friend back home realised from his letters that he was terribly unhappy. She was religious, and tried to help him when she wrote back. But Andrew was not having any of it. He just wanted to forget everything, have a good time, and perhaps get killed.

Then one day he was hit in the fighting. But the bullet did not kill him. It smashed his ankle.

In hospital he gradually realised that he would never be able to walk properly again. Far from getting himself killed, or being a hero, it looked as if he would be a cripple for the rest of his life. This was the last thing he had expected. For a young man it seemed to him worse than being killed. He became even more miserable.

While he was in hospital he had a lot of time to think. The nurses were nuns, and they were always cheerful and kind.

"How do you put up with all the unpleasant jobs you have to do?" Andrew asked one of them.

"Why, it is the love of Christ. You must know that, Andrew," she said simply.

This reminded him of his mother, who had died recently. She had believed very strongly in God. So for a short time after that, Andrew began to read the pocket Bible she had given him. However, as he got better, he gave it up.

Finally he arrived back in Holland, but he could still only hobble about. He was sent to a training-camp where injured soldiers were taught some kind of job, so that they could earn a living when they left the army. He was still very miserable, but tried to forget his sorrows by having a "good time" whenever he could. In fact, he celebrated his twenty-first birthday at that camp by getting completely drunk.

One day a pretty girl put her head round the door. All the boys in the room whistled! When the noise had died down she invited them to a "tent-meeting" that night.

Andrew and a number of the boys decided to go for fun. They guessed it was some sort of religious meeting, and they would enjoy themselves by making fun of the speaker. They also took plenty of drink along with them.

They certainly had fun. They caused so much disturbance that the speaker had to give up. Instead of preaching he prayed for the boys who were causing all the trouble. Then the people there began to sing the song "Let My People Go!" over and over again.

Strangely, after that meeting, Andrew felt different. The work he was being trained to do went better. He was not quite so miserable. Even more surprising, he began to read his Bible again. He also went to all the church services and meetings he could, even on week-nights!

He had begun to realise that the Bible had an answer to his problems. He was beginning to feel the power of God's love. In the end, after many months, he realised that he could become really happy again if he gave his life to God. He prayed very simply: "Lord, if You will show me the way, I will follow You. Amen."

Then he felt a peace he had never known before. All the bad feelings of the past were gone. He felt as if he were starting a brand-new life.

A new job

Not long after this he finally left the army and started a job. It was in a chocolate factory. Most of the people who worked there were girls, but not the kind he liked. Even he was shocked at the jokes some of them used to tell. They even made fun of a blind girl who worked there.

One day he met a girl in the factory who was different from the others. Andrew discovered that she was a Christian like himself. They decided to pray for the other girls, who could be so rude and thoughtless. They also tried to show the girls who told such unkind jokes that there is a better way to talk and live – the way of Jesus. To their amazement, after some months the very worst of all the girls became a Christian, and soon others followed.

One day the owner of the factory called Andrew into his office. He had noticed that Andrew was telling the other workers about Jesus. But instead of being angry, he offered Andrew a better job! He made him the personnel manager, who had the job of looking after all the workers in the factory.

All this time Andrew was himself learning more about the Christian faith. One day he went with a friend called Cornelius to a meeting in Amsterdam. At the end of the meeting the speaker said something unusual: "God is speaking to some young men here tonight. He wants you to give your whole life to serving Him as missionaries."

Andrew and his friend had never even thought of such a

thing before, but somehow they felt that God was speaking to them personally.

Afterwards Andrew wondered how he could become a missionary. It would mean going to another country to tell people about Jesus Christ. But he still could not even walk properly!

One day when he was thinking about this he decided not to make any more excuses. If God wanted him to be a missionary, he would become one, in spite of his bad ankle.

When he got up to walk he immediately felt a sharp pain. Then, when he put his foot to the ground again, he was amazed. He could walk like a normal person. Andrew did not understand how it had happened, yet he now knew he could become a missionary.

However, there was still another problem. Andrew and Cornelius had no training. In fact, they had had little education, because the war was on while they were at school. Then they heard of a place called a Bible School, at Glasgow in Scotland. This Bible School even accepted people who had not passed any exams and trained them to serve God as missionaries.

Learning to trust God

At the Bible School, the students learned not only what the Bible says, but how to put it into practice.

Jesus said, "Go into all the world and preach the Gospel." The Gospel tells the good news that Jesus Christ died for our sins, so that we can be forgiven and receive the gift of everlasting life.

Millions of people in the world have never heard this. So the students were taught how to preach the Gospel, and then they were sent out to do so among the people in Glasgow. They were also told which countries needed more missionaries.

Jesus taught his followers to trust God, their Heavenly

Father, for everything they might need while they are serving Him. So the students learned to pray and trust in God for everything – money, food, clothes, or anything else they needed in order to do God's work.

One day Andrew and the other students were given a pound each and told to go off for a month preaching the Gospel in different towns and villages in Scotland. They were not allowed to ask anyone for money or for anything else. Instead they had to pray for it. Then at the end they had to give the pound back again.

It sounded impossible, but they found that it worked. Every time they prayed, sooner or later someone gave them what they needed, or a letter with some money in it arrived from someone who knew nothing about their prayer.

This experience helped Andrew, for quite soon the money he had brought with him from Holland ran out. But he found that as long as he obeyed God, sooner or later he received whatever he needed, although sometimes God kept him waiting till the last moment.

The teachers as well as the students at the Bible School trusted God like this. And this is the way Andrew has lived ever since, simply trusting God.

The adventure begins

Andrew's course at the Bible School finished in the summer of 1955. Many of the students were already sure where God wanted them to serve Him – Africa, Asia or some other part of the world. But where did God want Andrew to go? He thought it might be Indonesia, where he had been a soldier, but he was not sure.

Then one day before he left the Bible School he came across a magazine. It had lots of pictures of countries like Russia and Poland. It said that life in these countries was very good because they had communist governments.

Communists say that their way of running a country is better than ours. In a communist country no one is allowed to become rich by owning a business. Instead, the Government owns all the shops, factories and farms, and the Government pays all the workers. Everyone has to do what the Communist Party says, even if they disagree with it.

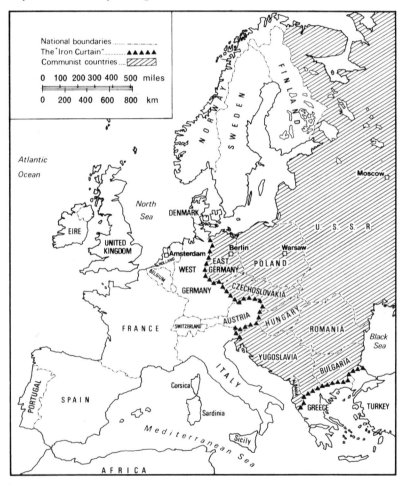

Europe, showing countries behind the "Iron Curtain"

8

Some people think that communism is a good idea, because it claims to look after the workers better. Other people say that communism takes away too much of people's freedom. Certainly a lot of people in communist countries end up in prison for things which we do not think are crimes.

Communism was started by two men called Karl Marx and Lenin. They both taught that there is no God, and that religion is a bad thing. So in communist countries Christians have a hard time. Often they cannot get good jobs. Many churches have been closed. There are few Bibles. Christians are put in prison or even tortured for their faith.

In the magazine that Andrew found, there were details of a big youth conference in Warsaw, the capital of Poland. It was organised to show people from other countries how good communism is. For some reason Andrew felt that he should write for more information. He explained in his letter that he was training to be a Christian missionary, but he would like to know more about life in communist countries.

To his surprise, he received a letter in reply saying that he would be welcome to attend the conference.

"Thank you for being here"

Warsaw had been badly damaged during the war, but by 1955 a lot had been rebuilt. Day after day Andrew and the other foreign visitors were shown streets of fine new buildings. They also had to sit through long speeches saying how good communism is, and how fine it would be if every country were communist. Andrew found it rather boring.

One day he managed to slip off by himself. He soon saw that not all the city was as fine as the parts they had been shown. In the back streets there were still plenty of poor people and war-damaged houses – just as there were in Britain and other countries at that time.

Easter service at a church in Moscow

On Sunday he decided to visit a church. It was not easy to find one, but at last he managed to do so. When he went in, the people realised at once that he was a foreigner. One or two of them could speak English, like Andrew. So afterwards they talked to him and answered his questions.

"Do you have freedom of religion?" he asked.

"Yes," they replied, "as long as we obey the Government's rules. . . ."

Andrew decided to visit another church. This time, when he was noticed by the people there, they invited him on to the platform to speak. First he brought them greetings from Christians in England and Holland. Then he preached. When he had finished, the pastor said, "We want to thank you for *being* here. Even if you had not said anything, it means so much to us to have a visitor. Sometimes we feel very alone in our struggle."

That made Andrew think. Was this the work that God wanted him to do? These Christians were struggling to keep their faith alive. Life was very hard for them. Was Andrew to help and encourage them?

Before he left Warsaw Andrew saw something else. One day there was a big parade. Hundreds of young people with red scarves marched through the main street. They were all singing communist songs. It took over fifteen minutes for them to pass by, because there were so many.

All these young people believed that communism is the answer to the world's problems. They were going to do all they could to convert the world to communism. They were willing to fight and die for their ideas.

Andrew was sure that these young people were wrong. He knew that the Christian way is better than that of communism. He was sure that he must do something about it.

When he returned to Holland he found that many people wanted to hear about his visit to a communist country. Some began to give him money so that he could make another journey to Eastern Europe. This time he went to Czechoslovakia, again with a party of tourists.

On Sunday he visited five churches in one day, and was asked to speak in four of them. Once again the Christians there were overjoyed to see him. But Andrew also found that they had a great need for Bibles. There were so few that, if one person had a Bible, he held it up high so that all those round him could read it as well! From that moment Andrew made up his mind to take as many Bibles as he could to Christians in communist countries.

The Hungarian revolt

Next autumn something happened which shook the whole of Europe. There was a revolt in Hungary. The people rebelled against their Russian masters, and called on other countries to help them. But none did. Soon the Russian tanks rolled into Hungary and crushed the revolt. Thousands of people fled from the country out of fear.

When these people reached the West, however, they had nowhere to live except in refugee camps. They had no work, money, food or clothes. Andrew decided to go and help in one of these refugee camps in Berlin. There he shared out food and clothes which had been given by people in Western Europe.

He also found that the refugees were very glad when he held services. For years these unhappy people had not been able to read the Bible or learn freely about Jesus. Now Andrew told them of God's love and power. As he did so, he saw their faces light up with new hope. This gave him great joy.

After doing this work for a while he finally received permission to visit another communist country, Yugoslavia. This time his friends gave him a small car. Now he could take some Bibles with him.

But there was a problem. If the frontier guards saw the Bibles, they would take them away. How could Andrew get the Bibles across the frontier?

"Lord, shut their eyes"

As Andrew approached the border he prayed:

"Lord, I believe you want me to take these Bibles into Yugoslavia, even if the Government does not. Please now shut the eyes of the guards, so that they will not see the Bibles."

At the frontier, the guards looked through his cases quickly. They must have seen some of the Bibles, but without realising what they were. God had answered Andrew's prayer, and the same thing has happened many times since.

That trip through Yugoslavia lasted seven weeks. Andrew drove his new car thousands of miles over all kinds of bad roads, and even cart-tracks. There were very few garages, and at that time Andrew knew little about cars. So he used to pray that God would keep the car going.

One day a motor mechanic heard about this. He came up to Andrew after a service and said, "I hear that you are praying about your car. Would you like me to look at it for you?"

"Yes, please," said Andrew.

The mechanic looked at the engine. He stared in amazement. "I never thought God could answer prayers like that," he said. "It is just impossible for this car to go. The air filter, the plugs, everything needs cleaning. I just can't believe it has kept running in this condition."

"But it has taken me thousands of miles," replied Andrew.

This answer to prayer helped the mechanic to believe in God much more firmly. He took the car to his yard, cleaned the engine, and changed the oil.

After that trip the way opened up for Andrew to visit more and more communist countries: Bulgaria, Romania, East Germany, Hungary, Albania. Everywhere it was the same story. The Christians were thrilled to have a visitor from the West. They needed all kinds of help but, most of all, Bibles.

Each country had its own problems. Even in the same country, Christians in some areas had more freedom than in others. Some could meet in church fairly freely, although they were short of Bibles and hymn-books. But others had to meet secretly in each other's homes, or even in the woods. And there, too, they were sometimes discovered and arrested.

On one occasion the police broke up a meeting in a home where Andrew was present. Andrew and the local Christian leader, who happened to be a university professor, were told to report to the police station the next morning. The little group of Christians prayed hard for them that night.

The next day, when Andrew and his friend turned up at the police station, they were told to wait. They waited a long time. In the end they learned that the police chief had been taken ill during the night! Andrew was allowed to go. His friend later lost his job at the university, but that was better than being put in prison, as he might have been.

Andrew had now been doing this work for two years. Each time he returned home he felt very lonely. He wished he could marry. But who would want to marry a person like him? He did not earn any money, he did dangerous work, and he was away travelling much of the time.

One day, as he was praying, he remembered the girl at the chocolate factory. Her name was Corry, and he had heard she was now a nurse. He decided to visit her. Gradually they fell in love. Andrew told her all the problems she would face

Russian Christians holding a service in the woods

if she married him. But she still said "Yes!" when he asked her. They got married.

Today they have five teen-age children. Of course, they all miss Andrew when he is away for so many months of the year.

Travelling has dangers as well. Late one night he was returning home along a narrow road in Holland. Suddenly a car came fast round a corner on the wrong side of the road.

Andrew thought he was going to die. There was a head-on collision. Yet Andrew was able to scramble out dazed, with little worse than some scratches and bruises.

Andrew has learned to trust God in every kind of danger and difficulty.

Russia

By this time Andrew had visited nearly all the communist countries in Europe. He had even made one short trip to Russia itself. Now he believed he must go back there, and take as many Bibles as possible.

Another Dutchman, called Hans, had joined him in the work, and they went together. Hans had even learned some Russian. They also had a larger car, and Hans was learning to drive. It is a long drive to Russia – from Amsterdam through Berlin and Warsaw to Moscow is about 2000 miles. Andrew was glad to have someone with him.

At the Russian frontier they prayed that the guards would not see the Bibles. All went well.

They reached Moscow. On Sunday they went to the Baptist church there. It was packed with 2000 people. There are three services every Sunday, and each one lasts for two or three hours.

Many people think that everyone in Russia is a communist and that no one there believes in God. This is very far from the truth. There are about 15 million members of the Communist Party out of 230 million people. There are probably about 60 million Christians. This is four times as many people as there are in the Communist Party!

Most Russian Christians belong to the Russian Orthodox Church (which is something like the Roman Catholic Church), while others are Baptists or Pentecostals or belong to other smaller groups. The churches are often packed with people. This is partly because many churches have been closed by the State, but it is also because so many people believe in God, and more are turning to God all the time.

Although there are many Christians in Russia, it is very difficult for them to get Bibles. The Government prints a few, but there are never enough for all the Christians who want one.

When Andrew and Hans went to the Baptist church in Moscow they met a man who had come 2000 miles from Siberia, in the hope of getting some Bibles in Moscow. He arrived there on the same day that Andrew and Hans brought their Bibles into the city, ready to give them away secretly. They gave him one, and said they would give him some more if he came back the next day.

They went to the church the next day, but the man from Siberia was not there. After some time the pastor of the church came. He was alone.

"I am sorry your Siberian friend cannot come," he said softly. "You see, one of the secret police saw him with you yesterday. Now he has been 'spoken to' by the police. He cannot come. Do you have something for him?"

Andrew explained that they had more Bibles. The pastor was silent, and then he showed them his hands.

"Do you see my finger-nails?" he asked. He had obviously been tortured. "I have spent my time in prison. If I am found with your Bibles I might be sent back. I cannot risk it again. But I will find someone who will take those Bibles."

The next day they drove to a spot right in the centre of Moscow. At the exact time arranged, another car drew up. Quickly they passed the parcels of Bibles to the people inside, and then the other car drove off.

When the Russian Christians have a Bible, they really use it. Sometimes they even copy it out by hand, so that others may have a part. A girl called Aida Skripnikova wrote out

17

some Bible verses on picture postcards, and gave them to passers-by on the street. For this she was put in prison. She has now been in prison three times.

A young soldier called Ivan Moiseyev gained such faith from the Bible that in 1972 he suffered torture and death rather than give up his faith.

Officially the Russian Government allows freedom of religion, as long as people keep it to themselves. But once they start sharing their faith with others, especially young people, they get into trouble. Even today there are many Russian Christians in prison, or in exile, in Siberia.

Aida Skripnikova

Ivan Moiseyev ("Vanya")

The invasion of Czechoslovakia

One day in 1968 Andrew had just returned from a journey. Then news came that the Russians had sent their soldiers and tanks into Czechoslovakia. A brave leader called Alexander Dubček (pronounced "Doobcheck") had tried to give his people more freedom. But the Russians would not let him. That is why they sent in their army.

Immediately all Western visitors, and many Czech citizens, tried to escape. The border crossings to the West were jammed with people trying to get through before the Russians closed the frontier.

Andrew, however, immediately loaded his car with Bibles and drove to Czechoslovakia. He knew he might not get out again, but he felt he must get some Bibles into the country before the frontier was closed.

When he arrived he gave out the Bibles. He also encouraged the Christians to trust God. One day he saw a rough poster that someone had put up. It was a drawing of Jesus on the cross, with two Russian soldiers on guard. That shows how the Czech people, at the time of their trouble, remembered the sufferings of Jesus.

Andrew arrived home safely. But this was the last time that he went to Eastern Europe. Now he is too well known there. It would not be safe for him, nor for the people he visited, if he went again. But his work has not stopped.

The work grows

As Andrew told people in Holland and other countries about the Christians in Eastern Europe and Russia, many began to pray. They gave money for more Bibles. Then other young men like Hans began to travel to communist countries themselves. Between them they formed a team.

To keep people informed, Andrew and his team started

a magazine called "Open Doors". In 1967 an American author helped Andrew to write a book about his experiences. It was called *God's Smuggler*.

More helpers and more money came. The teams were able to take other things besides Bibles: clothes, medicines, tape-recorders, typewriters and even motor cars – anything which

Brother Andrew

would help the Christians in Eastern Europe to serve God better.

Meanwhile Andrew began visiting other countries, such as Cuba, Vietnam and even China. At that time China was almost completely closed to foreigners. Many people told Andrew that he would not be able to go there. But Andrew believes that nothing is impossible if God has told us to do it. So he simply prayed and trusted God to give him an "open door" into China – and He did! Since then, other Christians have visited China also. They have found that the Christian church is alive and growing. In fact, right now the Christians in China need a million Chinese Bibles. So Brother Andrew and his fellow-workers are doing their best, with God's help, to supply them.

Andrew is still visiting countries where life is hard for Christians. He wants to see the Gospel preached in every country, just as Jesus commanded. To him there are no "closed doors". Jesus came into the world and died to bring us God's love. So we should be willing to live, and even die for Him.

BIOGRAPHICAL NOTES

Andrew's Dutch name is very difficult for English people to say. So he is widely known as "Brother Andrew".

He was born at a small village in North Holland. Holland was occupied by the Germans from May 1940 till the end of the war in 1945.

Andrew joined the Dutch army in January 1946, and served in Indonesia from November 1946 till he was wounded in February 1949.

He became a Christian in January 1950. He worked in the chocolate factory from 1950 to 1953, when he went to the Missionary Training College of the Worldwide Evangelization Crusade, in Glasgow. He stayed there for two years.

He first visited a communist country, Poland, in 1955. The Hungarian revolt took place in 1956. After working for some months in a refugee camp in Berlin he continued his visits to other communist countries in Eastern Europe.

Andrew's first visit to Russia was in 1957. His last visit to a communist country in Europe was to Czechoslovakia at the time of the Russian invasion in 1968.

Meanwhile Andrew had already begun visiting countries outside Europe: China and Vietnam in 1965, Cuba in 1966, Uganda in 1976.

He organised some special conferences to encourage Christian work in some of these countries: "Love China" in 1975, and "Love Africa" in 1978.

Today Andrew spends most of his time travelling round the world challenging young Christians to help the Church in countries where there is persecution, and to preach the Gospel in every land as Christ commanded.

THINGS TO DO

A Test yourself

Here are some short questions. See if you can remember the answers from what you have read. Then write them down in a few words.

1 In what country was Andrew born?
2 In which year did the Germans invade Holland?
3 Why did Andrew hate being a soldier?
4 What was Andrew's first simple prayer, when he gave his life to God?
5 Where did Andrew start work after he left the army?
6 Where was the Bible School that Andrew went to?
7 Which was the first communist country that Andrew visited?
8 How many people attended the service at the Baptist church in Moscow?
9 Why was the Russian girl, Aida Skripnikova, put in prison?
10 Why did Andrew believe he could get into China when it seemed impossible?

B Think through

These questions need longer answers. Think about them, and then try to write two or three sentences in answer to each one. You may look up the story again to help you.

1 What kind of things did Andrew learn at the Bible School?
2 How did Andrew first get the idea of going to a communist country?
3 What difficulties do Christians in communist countries have?
4 Why was the pastor in Moscow afraid to take Andrew's Bibles?
5 Give an example of a time when Andrew prayed and God answered his prayer.

C Talk about

Here are some questions for you to discuss together. Try to give reasons for what you say or think. Try to find out the different opinions which people have about each question.

1 Why did Andrew and his friends make up the motto, "Be smart. Go crazy!"? Why did Andrew first make fun of religion but later become a Christian? Do you think that, deep down, other young people would like to know God, even though they make fun of religion like Andrew did?
2 Look up Matthew, chapter 6, verse 33. Is it really possible for a

24

Christian to obtain the things he needs by praying for them? How do you explain the "answers" to Andrew's prayers? Can other people have similar experiences?

3 Why do you think so many people in communist countries believe in God, when everything possible is done to persuade them that God does not exist? Why are some of them willing to go to prison or die for their faith?

4 Why are Christians persecuted in some countries? Why are they sometimes laughed at in this country? Why was Jesus put to death when he had done nothing wrong? The Bible says that God loves the world, so why do some people hate or fear Him?

D Find out

Choose one or two of the subjects below and find out all you can about them. History books, geography books and newspapers may be useful. Perhaps you can use reference books in your library to look up some of the names and places. Older people may be able to answer some of the questions from memory.

1 *Holland*
   (a) Draw a map of Holland, and put in the towns of Amsterdam, Den Haag (The Hague) and Rotterdam. Draw in the River Rhine.
   (b) Find out why the country is so flat, and why there are so many dikes and ditches.
   (c) What things is Holland famous for?
   (d) Find out the stories of Anne Frank and Corrie ten Boom during the war.
   (e) Find out what happened at Arnhem in 1944.

2 *Russia*
   (a) Find out the proper name of this country today.
   (b) Who used to rule the country before the Revolution in 1917?
   (c) Who was Lenin? Who was Karl Marx?
   (d) Find out about the way the Russians defended Stalingrad against Hitler's armies.
   (e) Find out about some of the people who are in prison today for trying to get more freedom in Russia.

3 *Eastern Europe*
   (a) What is the "Iron Curtain"? Find out which countries are behind it. How did they become communist countries?
   (b) Find out about the Hungarian revolt, and about the invasion of

Czechoslovakia. In what brave way did some students show that they did not want the Russians, even though they did not fight?

4   *Christians in Eastern Europe*

   (a) Find out all you can about Christians in Eastern Europe, including the following people: Ivan Moiseyev ("Vanya"), Aida Skripnikova, Georgi Vins. Find out about organisations that are helping people like this, such as "Open Doors" and Keston College.

USEFUL INFORMATION

Addresses

"Open Doors"   Keston College
P.O. Box 6   Heathfield Road
Standlake   Keston, Kent
Witney, Oxon   BR2 6BA.
OX8 7SP.

N.B. Remember to enclose a stamped, addressed envelope for the reply. A postal order for 50p would also be helpful, if you want plenty of material.

More books to read

Aida of Leningrad, by Michael Bourdeaux (Mowbray's) (T).
The Answer to Moscow's Bible, by Richard Wurmbrand (Hodder & Stoughton) (T).
Discretion and Valour, by Trevor Beeson (Collins) (T).
God's Smuggler, by Brother Andrew (Hodder & Stoughton) (T).
The Hiding Place, by Corrie ten Boom (Hodder & Stoughton) (T).
Ivan and the Daring Escape, by Myrna Grant (Kingsway) (P).
The Secret Room: Corrie ten Boom, by David Wallington (R.M.E.P.) (P).
A Song in Siberia, by Anita and Peter Deyneka (Collins) (T).
Three Generations of Suffering, by Georgi Vins (Hodder & Stoughton) (T).
Trial of Faith, The Story of Richard Wurmbrand, by Roger Owen (R.M.E.P.) (P).

(T) = suitable for teachers and older pupils
(P) = suitable for younger pupils

Films

The Bitter Cup (45 min), black and white. A film of the Church in Russia. Available from Keston College.
Faithfulness (45 min), black and white. A reconstruction of the trial of Georgi Vins. Available from Keston College.
More Than Meets the Eye (25 min), colour. A film about the work of "Open Doors". Available for showing by a representative of "Open Doors".
Prisonland (30 min), black and white. A documentary, partly filmed in Russia. Available from The Women's Campaign for Soviet Jewry, 148 Glanville Road, London NW2.

N.B. Most of these films are more suitable for older pupils.

Slides

The Suffering Church in Eastern Europe (25 min), colour. An introduction to the Church in the nine countries of Eastern Europe.

The Church in the Soviet Union (25 min), colour. A closer look at the Church in the largest of the Eastern European countries.

My Brother's Slides (10 min), colour. A child's eye view of Eastern Europe. All three sets of slides available with cassette or reel commentaries from "Open Doors".